Mindful Yoga Therapy
GIVE BACK YOGA FOUNDATION

Suzanne Manafort and Robin Gilmartin

GIVE BACK YOGA FOUNDATION™

Published by Give Back Yoga Foundation
Boulder, CO

Published by the Give Back Yoga Foundation, Boulder, CO
for Mindful Yoga Therapy.

Mindful Yoga Therapy is a non-profit organization that is fiscally sponsored by The Give Back Yoga Foundation. Our mission is to help Veterans to find a calm and steady body/mind to continue productive and peaceful lives through the support of the mindful practices of yoga. Our programs are clinically tested. We've been working with Veterans with Post Traumatic Stress (PTS) in residential treatment programs and in outpatient programs for several years. This work led to the development of Mindful Yoga Therapy. www.mindfulyogatherapy.org

Give Back Yoga Foundation believes in making yoga available to those who might not otherwise have the opportunity to experience the transformational benefits of this powerful practice. We do this by supporting and funding certified yoga teachers in all traditions to offer the teachings of yoga to under-served and under-resourced socioeconomic segments of the community and inspire grassroots social change and community cooperation. www.givebackyoga.org

Edited by Patty Townsend, Amy Lawson and Rob Schware.
Photos by Eric Ramm. Graphic design by Susanne Murtha.

ISBN: 978-0-9888138-3-0

Library of Congress Control Number: 2015933329

Printed in the United States of America

25 24 23 22 21 20 19 18 17 16 15   3 4 5 6 7 8 9 10

Our Gratitude

We are so grateful to be surrounded by so many amazing, kind and generous people. We would like to acknowledge their support.

Thank you to Patty Townsend for giving us a yoga home to learn and grow in and for teaching us your wealth of knowledge and experience. Thank you for all you have contributed to this project.

Thank you to Beryl Bender Birch for all your support, for being the mountain that you are and teaching us how it's done.

Thank you to Rob Schware for everything and more. You are the man!

Thank you to the Give Back Yoga Foundation and its board for all of your support.

Thank you to Sven and Christina for posing for the beautiful photos.

Last but certainly not least, thank you to all Veterans for your dedication, bravery and all the sacrifices that you have made for us.

This project was supported and funded by the
Give Back Yoga Foundation

Table of Contents

FORWARD

Mindful Yoga Therapy for Veterans is a powerful tool to promote tranquility and healing for the body. In this succinct manual, my dear friend Suzanne Manafort introduces the practice of yoga to our heroes. The wisdom contained in this book is now a significant part of my personal and professional life.

Throughout the years, I have combined my military career with a fulfilling yoga practice. My warrior quests have taken me all over the world. I have served in two major armed conflicts and worked at the largest center for military strategy, the Pentagon. Despite my triumphs and adventures, I have also experienced a few downfalls. Due to the high demands of my military service, I too, have found myself depressed and stressed for periods of time. Additionally, I have seen the reality of Post Traumatic Stress (PTS) up close and personally: in friends, co-workers, and my brothers and sisters in uniform. It is not easy when someone you love falls into a dark place of isolation, anxiety, and despair.

As a yoga teacher and a military veteran, I wanted to connect the dots and develop my own conclusions for what I believe to be an effective, accepted, and comfortable yoga approach to support our veterans and their families. While working on my advanced yoga certification, I decided to write my final thesis on "Yoga for Veterans Coping with PTS." As I embarked on this journey, I met wonderful teachers, and learned and experienced different methods. I have no doubt that Mindful Yoga Therapy is by far the soundest approach available to the veteran community. The combination of intentional practices of breathing, asana, yoga nidra, meditation, and gratitude offer a wide range of possibilities to teachers and veteran practitioners. Moreover, I admire Suzanne's efforts to promote the program at minimal or no cost to veterans. Her love for our heroes, dedication, and hard work in partnership with the Give Back Yoga Foundation has made the program widely accessible to our community.

I am happy to say that I have successfully included Mindful Yoga Therapy principles in the yoga classes I teach at the Pentagon Athletic Center and at various workshops and Wounded Warrior Camps. For a teacher, there is nothing more rewarding than completing a hero's yoga practice and feeling the joy and tranquility permeating the space. As a veteran practicing yoga, the feeling of connection to other warriors, and the sense of being safe and grounded while nurturing rest and healing, is priceless.

Mindful Yoga Therapy focuses on supporting veterans, but I truly believe this approach also serves as a physical and mental resilience-building tool for people from all walks of life. By applying Suzanne's "toolbox" while cultivating a steady yoga practice, you will experience a wonderful and positive transformation for living well and better! It is my honor to write the forward to this practice guide.

— Dulia Mora-Turner
RYT500 Yoga Teacher and Captain, United States Air Force

Introduction

There is a look that crosses the faces of some veterans when they first hear about yoga for veterans with post-traumatic stress (PTS). The look says, "You've got to be kidding!" Another veteran may see that look and jump in, saying, "I know what you're thinking and I felt the same way. It took me a while to even give it a chance, but you know, it really helps me with my PTS."

It's important to understand some basics about yoga. Yoga is not a religion or a cult or a political movement. It's not exclusive to any particular group of people. Spiritual men and women have practiced yoga for several thousand years. It has been used to train elite athletes, warriors, and martial artists. Many veterans, both those with and without post-traumatic stress, are now using yoga techniques to build strength and resilience and to heal from the traumas of war. Yoga is now offered at many military installations, and many treatment programs within the VA system include some form of yoga or mindfulness practices along with traditional psychotherapies and medications. Yoga practices typically include breathing techniques, physical postures and mindful movement, guided rest, and meditation.

What Is Mindful Yoga Therapy?

Mindful Yoga Therapy is a collection of simple but effective practices that we have adapted and clinically tested specifically for military service members and veterans recovering from post-traumatic stress and stress associated with civilian readjustment. These practices can be used to enhance the health of the body and mind, regardless of physical limitations or psychological distress.

In Mindful Yoga Therapy, you will learn many different yoga "practices." Each practice is a "tool" veterans can use to cope with post-traumatic stress. Together, these tools form a comprehensive system—a toolbox—that will carry veterans into a life of strength and resilience.

You have choices about how you use these tools. For example, while practicing meditation, some people like to sit in a chair while others prefer to sit on a cushion on the floor. Some veterans like to practice breathing techniques while seated, and others prefer to be reclined. Mindful Yoga Therapy is about finding out what works best for you.

Many of the veterans with post-traumatic stress who have learned and now practice these techniques report improved sleep, better focus and concentration, less irritability and anger, and overall more enjoyment in their daily lives. Mindful Yoga Therapy seems to be especially helpful for veterans who are also participating in evidence-based psychotherapy treatment for post-traumatic stress. (Note: we do not advocate Mindful Yoga Therapy as a replacement for post-traumatic stress treatment. It may be used successfully in addition to traditional therapies.)

Post-Traumatic Stress and Its Symptoms

Post-traumatic stress, also called Post-Traumatic Stress Disorder (PTSD), is one of the mental health condition caused by an external event (trauma). Post-traumatic stress is a natural reaction to unnatural circumstances. Traumatic events include military combat, accidents, natural disasters, or violent events such as child abuse or sexual assault. Traumas can shatter a person's sense of safety and make it difficult to trust others again. Veterans with post-traumatic stress avoid doing things or going places where they are not in control of their surroundings. These effects can greatly disrupt daily living. Sometimes there is also a fear of being overwhelmed by unwanted thoughts or feelings. Does any of this sound familiar to you?

There are four symptom "clusters," or groupings of symptoms, in post-traumatic stress. They are **Arousal**, **Intrusion**, **Avoidance**, and **Negative Cognitions and Moods**. Let's look at each cluster individually.

Arousal Symptoms

Arousal reactions are all about survival. During combat or other traumatic events, survival reactions take over. These reactions are activated automatically through the body's sympathetic nervous system, which is also known as "fight or flight." When activated by the amygdala (the brain's "emergency dispatcher"), the sympathetic nervous system instantly responds with physiological changes affecting many parts of the body. Again, the purpose of these changes is to maximize our chances for survival.

We all know what fight or flight feels like, but we may not be aware of all that is happening within us.

Physiological Reactions during Fight or Flight Response:
• Respiration and heart rate increase
• Pupils dilate to take in more light and visual information
• Arteries dilate and veins constrict to increase blood flow
• The body releases glucose (sugar) as a quick energy source
• Blood, oxygen, and sugar are rushed to large muscle groups
• Non-critical functions such as digestion are slowed or halted
• Natural opiates are released and capillaries are constricted in case of injury
• Emotions vary, but typically include anger, fear, or a sense of exhilaration.

These and other physical and mental changes happen automatically and with incredible efficiency to keep us alive.

But here's the problem: having chronic post-traumatic stress means that the sympathetic nervous system is overly active even when there is no real threat or danger. One veteran described hypervigilance, one of the arousal symptoms, as "being constantly on guard and never on stand-down." Arousal can also interfere with sleep, lead to feelings of anger or irritability, make it hard to concentrate, and cause startle reactions.

Over time, physical problems can also develop as a result of an overactive sympathetic nervous system. These include hypertension, tension headaches, muscular pain, gastrointestinal complaints (acid reflux, stomach upset, and diarrhea), stress-related weight gain, and an increased risk for type 2 diabetes.

Arousal Symptoms
- Irritability or aggression
- Self-destructiveness or recklessness
- Hypervigilance
- Exaggerated startle response
- Difficulty concentrating
- Sleep disturbance

Intrusive Symptoms

Intrusive symptoms include intrusive thoughts and feelings, flashbacks, and nightmares related to the trauma you experienced. It's important to understand the connection between intrusive symptoms and arousal symptoms in post-traumatic stress. Have you noticed that when you are really stressed out, on guard, or angry about something, you are more likely to have intrusive thoughts about the past, feelings of distress, or even flashbacks? Daily stress that triggers fight or flight reactions often increases intrusive symptoms. You may also be more likely to have trauma nightmares when you have felt stressed out during the day.

Intrusive Symptoms
- Recurrent and intrusive memories
- Trauma nightmares
- Dissociative reactions, such as flashbacks
- Intense distress when exposed to trauma reminders
- Physical reaction to trauma-related stimuli

Intrusive symptoms, such as intrusive thoughts, nightmares, and flashbacks, can also increase arousal and result in a "feedback loop" or what is sometimes called the Cycle of Stress:

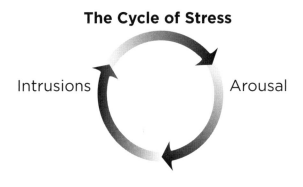

The Cycle of Stress

Intrusions   Arousal

Avoidance Symptoms

Avoidance symptoms include efforts to avoid thoughts, feelings, situations, memories, or reminders of past traumas. Shutting off feelings at the time of a trauma made sense; you could not afford to stop what you were doing to "feel your feelings." Reaction and survival took first priority. Once you are out of the war zone, however, emotional numbing creates problems. While it may be familiar and comfortable, numbing may prevent you from connecting with other people and living life more fully. Many trauma survivors also use substances to help numb feelings and try to forget their experiences. Some veterans keep busy all the time or work long hours to avoid having down time during which painful memories and feelings come up. Dissociating, "checking out" mentally, or feeling disconnected from others are also common avoidance symptoms.

Avoidance Symptoms
- Persistent effort to avoid thoughts or feelings about the trauma
- Persistent effort to avoid trauma-related external reminders (such as people, places, activities, objects or situations)

At a deep level, traumatic experiences affect the way we think about the world, other people, and ourselves. As one veteran put it, "I came home a different person. I know I love my family but I can't really show it yet. I don't know why I made it back and I feel like I don't deserve to be here. I don't trust anyone and I don't fit in any more." Negative cognitions and moods include negative beliefs about yourself and other people, including judging yourself and others harshly. You may have persistent feelings of guilt and shame. You may feel a lot of anger or fear, but have difficulty expressing positive emotions like love and gratitude. These feelings can lead to more guilt and shame, convincing you that you are un-deserving.

Seeking support from others who understand and seeking help from professionals are important steps toward recovery. In addition, Mindful Yoga Therapy may also help you find some peace within yourself and aid in the recovery process.

Negative Cognition and Mood Symptoms:

- Inability to recall the traumatic event
- Negative beliefs and expectations about yourself or the world ("I am bad" or "the world is completely dangerous")
- Distorted sense of blame (blaming yourself or others for things outside of your control)
- Negative trauma-related emotions (fear, horror, anger, guilt or shame)
- Lack of interest in activities
- Feeling detached from others
- Difficulty experiencing positive emotions

How Can Mindful Yoga Therapy Help with Post-traumatic Stress?

Mindful Yoga Therapy does not set out to change who you are or what you believe. You will not be told what you should think or how you should feel about anything. Yoga is an ancient tradition that values *acceptance*; this includes acceptance of each unique individual with a unique set of life circumstances. The tradition of yoga also values *interconnection* between all people, despite our many differences.

Each yoga practice you will learn in Mindful Yoga Therapy can help manage the effects of post-traumatic stress on your body, mind, and sense of well-being. You'll learn how to develop mindfulness, or paying attention to the present moment, and observing without judgment. The mindful movement and breathing practices will help restore balance in your nervous system and cultivate a calmer state of mind. A resting practice called yoga nidra further aids in balancing your nervous system and leads to the deepest levels of relaxation in the body and mind. Through the practice of meditation you may find a feeling of peacefulness, which may then carry over into your daily life. Each yoga practice ends with the simple act of gratitude, or silent acknowledgement of something you are grateful for that day.

Acceptance, which in yoga is called *santosha*, begins with accepting yourself as you are. Practicing self-acceptance may help you feel more accepting of others. Through the practices of acceptance, mindfulness, and gratitude, you may discover a sense of inner peace and calm, and begin to feel a greater connection to the world. You may also find over time that negative emotions like anger, shame, and fear gradually diminish, and positive emotions like acceptance, love, and gratitude increase.

The Tool Box

The practice of yoga is thousands of years old and consists of a variety of different practices. The practice that we see most often called yoga in our society is usually just the postures and movement practices, or *asana*. The ancient practice of yoga can include much more that that. There are also breathing practices, yoga nidra (a resting practice), meditation, and many more.

Because we are all individuals, some of the yoga practices work better for some people and some of the symptoms of PTSD than others. With this in mind, we present these practices as a *Tool Box* with a set of individual tools in it that are always available to you. We invite you to try each of these tools and practice those you find helpful. You may want to try different tools at different times.

Many teachers use the language of Sanskrit to teach yoga. We present the original Sanskrit names of each of the practices in parentheses below.

The Tool Box consists of:

Breathing (Pranayama)
  Cellular Breath
  Three-part Breath
  Victorious Breath (Ujjayi)
  Alternate-nostril Breath (Nadi Shodhana)

Mindful movement connected with breath (Asana)

Yoga Nidra

Meditation

Gratitude

This practice guide will address and explain each of these practices separately.

Breathing Practices (Pranayama)

The breath is where it begins. Connection with the breath is the backbone of any yoga practice and may be the most important gift you can give yourself.

We intuitively know that breath is the key to helping us find our way to comfort, calmness, and wellbeing. When someone becomes anxious or is in a stressful situation, we say "take a breath" or "breathe."

Our hearts beat continuously, our gastrointestinal tracts digest our food, our kidneys filter our blood and control our blood pressure, our hair and nails grow, our skin protects, our immune system fights infections and disease, our liver helps clean our blood as it moves through our body, and all of these organs and systems work together to keep us alive and well. And we have little or no conscious control over any of it! Respiration is really the only basic physiological function that is under both conscious and unconscious control. If we don't think about breathing, we breathe. If we think about breathing, we breathe.

We can do things to make these parts work better, such as exercising and eating right, but we can't just stop our heartbeat. We can't increase the rate at which we digest food with just conscious thought. *We can, however, control our breath.* Our ability to control our breath, or the rate at which we breathe and how deeply we breathe, is intricately tied to our ability to exert control over our thoughts, feelings, and behaviors. Essentially, we can use our breathing practices to help regulate how we feel and move through the world. Our ability to use breath in this way is a uniquely human quality.

Again, breathing techniques are used to cleanse, calm, and strengthen the nervous system, and thus increase vitality. Breathing is commonly used as an anxiety management technique. Breathing practices are also used as a tool to cultivate greater mental control over our emotions and our reactions to them. The use of slow and conscious breathing balances the nervous system, initiates the relaxation response and grounds us. The nervous system is further balanced as we use our breath in coordination with the yoga postures and movements. Breath can be a bridge between the body and mind.

Although these practices are subtle, they are very powerful. We recommend that all the practices be done as nose breathing only, with your mouth closed. No breath retentions are used in any of these breathing practices.

We will explore:

Cellular Breath
Cellular Breath is a wonderful journey inward that allows us to stay present and grounded. It also allows us to find the healing qualities of the breath. We become able to feel how our whole body is actually breathing as every cell receives oxygen from the breath.

Three-part Breath
Three-part Breath helps us bring more breath into our body by fully using our lungs, allowing us to calm our nervous system and find a more peaceful and perhaps a more restful place. Breath is energy, and Three-part Breath helps to ensure that we are getting all the fresh life force and vitality we need into our bodies with the breath. It is not unusual to find that some people in our society are only using the top portion of their lungs. This practice teaches us to use the entire lung, which allows more breath to move through the whole body.

Alternate-nostril Breath (Nadi Shodhana)
Science shows us that initiating breath in nostrils individually can help to balance the parasympathetic and sympathetic nervous systems. *Alternate-nostril Breath* can be a profoundly soothing practice.

Victorious Breath (Ujjayi)

It has been said that this *Victorious Breath* strengthens and tones the nervous system. This practice will allow you to sip the breath in and out more slowly and wash it through your whole body. This is the breathing technique we will use in our yoga postures practice. It is both enlivening and soothing. The overall effect is deeply calming and centering.

These breathing practices can be explored on the following pages, as downloads, or streamed on our website. They are from the CD **"Breathe In, Breathe Out."** Instructions for the download are on the inside back cover of this practice guide.

Cellular Breath

You may begin lying down with some support under your knees, such as a pillow or a rolled-up blanket.

Close your eyes if that feels possible. If not, just lower and soften your gaze.

Start by just observing your breath as if it is an exploration.

Notice how your breath feels today. It may feel deep and rich or it may feel shallow and light.

There is no right or wrong, so just observe. The purpose is to observe what today feels like, without judgment.

Bring your awareness to the base of your nostrils, right where the breath enters. Notice the sensation of it entering and exiting. Notice that it may be cool as it enters and warm as it exits. Allow yourself to feel this.

Draw your awareness in a little deeper and notice how the breath feels on the inside of your nostrils. Perhaps it is soft and fluffy, like velvet or cotton candy. You may also notice that your breath swirls its way in, and this may feel good. Take a moment here.

Now can you draw your awareness inward even deeper? Feel how your breath makes its way in through the nostrils and all the way into your lungs. Stay with this for several breaths. Maybe you can even imagine that the breath flows like a fluid as it makes its way in and then back out of your body.

Do you notice how your lungs expand when you inhale and condense when you exhale?

The next time you inhale and your lungs expand, imagine that the oxygen washes from your lungs into your bloodstream. From your bloodstream, the oxygen makes its way to all your organs and all your tissues, and to every single cell in your body. Imagine that every cell in your body is expanding and condensing individually with each breath.

Just stay with these pure sensations and images and allow the breath to wash through you and nourish your cells, tissues, and organs.

If you like, you can focus on one specific area that may be troublesome. As you bring your focus to this area, treat your awareness as if it were a sponge. Every time you inhale, the sponge brings in new and fresh oxygen that washes through you and when you exhale it sends out the unneeded, unwanted or waste. This sponging can be used in one specific area of your body, or as full body awareness.

Take as much time here as needed.

Three-part Breath

It may be helpful to know that our lungs are big, football-sized organs inside our ribcage. They have three lobes on one side and two lobes on the other. For this exploration we divide the lungs into three parts on both sides and call them top lungs, middle lungs and bottom lungs. We will also explore bringing the breath to the bottom lungs first, drawing our attention upward to the middle lungs, and finally to the top lungs.

Please begin in a reclining posture, preferably on the floor. If you need some support you can place a bolster or rolled up blanket under your knees.

This exploration begins with just noticing your breath. Allow your-self to notice the inhale and the exhale. It is important not to judge the way you are breathing. You will learn to bring breath through your whole body as your practice continues.

Bring your fingers to the top of your collarbones and place your fin-gertips in the hollows at the tops of the collarbones. This is the top of the lungs. As you take a very large inhale see if you can feel the top of the lungs puff up under your fingers like a balloon inflating.

Next bring your hands to the middle of your ribcage or even under your armpits. As you inhale, see if you can notice how your ribcage expands three dimensionally as your lungs fill, and notice how they condense on the exhale. This is the action of the middle lung.

Finally bring your hands to your lower ribcage. As you inhale this time, see if you feel the expand and condense of your bottom lungs.

Now rest your hands down by your sides.

Start by just taking a natural breath (an inhale and an exhale).

The next inhale should be very slow. As you inhale draw your breath first into the bottom lungs, slowly bring it up to the middle lungs, and finally fill up as you bring breath to the top lungs. Then exhale fully. Take a natural breath.

Repeat four more times, being mindful to take a natural breath between each *Three-part Breath*.

After completing five Three-part Breaths, close your eyes for a moment and notice how you feel. Compare this to how you felt before you started the practice. Again, we do not recommend breath retentions in this practice.

Alternate-nostril Breathing (Nadi Shodhana)

Science has shown us that we breathe dominantly in one nostril over the other and that the dominant side changes throughout the day. *Alternate Nostril Breathing* practice, or Nadi Sodhana, helps us breathe through both nostrils at the same time. Finding balance in the breath lets us find balance in the parasympathetic and sympathetic nervous systems.

This practice may be done reclining or seated. Find a comfortable place. If you are seated, plant your feet firmly on the earth. Close your eyes if that feels comfortable, but if it doesn't just try to lower your eyes and soften your gaze.

This practice begins again with just noticing the breath. This is always a great place to start. You may notice that it is repeated at the beginning of each practice. It's a great checking in point. How does my breath feel today? It allows you to settle in and there is a bit of comfort in your breath's own unique rhythm.

Take a few natural inhales and exhales with your mouth closed. Then take a large inhale and exhale fully though both nostrils. Feel the sensation of the breath in your nostrils.

Now, take your awareness primarily to your left nostril. The next inhale will be initiated in your left nostril. Allow your awareness to cross over the bridge of your nose and exhale through the right nostril.

Your next inhale will be felt with all of your awareness in your right nostril. Cross over the bridge of your nose and exhale through your left nostril.

This is one complete round. Remember, all you need to do is shift sides after each inhalation.

Try beginning your practice with five to ten rounds.

Allow yourself to come back to natural breathing and notice the effects of this practice. You may notice that you are breathing through both nostrils at the same time.

Take a few minutes to feel the results of this practice.

Victorious Breath (Ujjayi)

This breathing practice can be done several ways. It can be used as a strong, powerful, and heating breath or it can be done in a soft, slow, steady, and calming way. We will be doing a soft version without retentions.

You will also be trying to create evenness in your breath. For example, you may notice that your inhale is a little shorter than your exhale. Or that your exhale is slightly more exaggerated than your inhale. In this practice you will be trying to even out the inhale and exhale.

This practice is done through the nose with your mouth closed and with a bit of constriction in the back of the throat. It has an audible sound to it. It is sometimes referred to as ocean breath.

Start this exploration by imagining that you have a mirror in your hand. If you were going breathe on that mirror with the intention of fogging it up, you might open your mouth and breath on the mirror with a sound that sounds like ......HA.

Now, try this again, but this time close your mouth in the middle of the breath, and you may feel a bit of constriction at the back of your throat that creates a soft, audible sound.

Can you now do that with your mouth closed and do it on both your inhale and exhale?

Once this is established, start breathing with this soft sound and pay attention to the length of your inhale and exhale. Begin to create balance in the two.

Take a few moments to just breathe.

This breath can be taken with you wherever you go. It is a great tool to use in times of stress or anxiety. It will keep you present in this very moment and create a calming effect.

Mindful Movement and Postures (Asana)

Asana, or postures combined with movement and breath, is the practice almost everyone thinks of when they think of "yoga." This ancient practice is full of wisdom. Although the side effects of asana will give you strong muscles and keep you in shape, there is so much more to this practice than just physical exercise.

In the tradition of Embodyoga®, which is the foundation of Mindful Yoga Therapy, there are several principles that seem to aid in the recovery of PTS when accompanied by psychotherapy.

Support Precedes Action

We begin with *support precedes action* because support precedes any effective movement, non-movement, or action. It is important to know that you have the support you need before you make any move forward, take your next step in life, or even just move into a yoga posture. In other words, support precedes everything!

We have provided specific postures and techniques to help you find a connection to earth with your feet and even your hands when they are on the earth. The grounding connection to earth lets you know that you have the support that you need to move forward safely and with stability. This earthy, grounded feeling provides steadiness, a calm presence, and a sense of ease. With continued practice you may find new sensations of having support under you in many different areas of your body. You may begin to spontaneously initiate movement from these supports. When you know where your support is coming from, you find more comfort. This concept may apply in many areas of life—and we know it applies in our yoga practice.

Finding this connection, or relationship with earth, may help you begin to find a renewed relationship with yourself as well. Finding and nurturing this relationship with yourself, and feeling fully supported by the earth under you, will allow you to begin to explore your relationship with others too. Yoga offers us choice in our actions. Each of us takes our own time in coming into a deeper relationship with earth, with self, and with others. There is no timetable except for your own comfort. You're the boss in this!

We present the following supports in alphabetical order. Each one is equally important.

Acceptance

Your yoga practice will help you learn to practice *acceptance*. Acceptance of what is and where we actually are—in our mind and body—at each new moment and each new day, is an important principle in yoga practice. But it isn't always easy!

You may step on your yoga mat today and have an amazing practice that feels so good that you can't wait to do it again tomorrow. When tomorrow arrives, you may have an entirely different experience. You may have physical limitations that don't allow you to do the full expression of the posture. You may be tired, or just not feeling good. In practicing acceptance of how we actually are and feel each day, we just proceed on with our practice. Acceptance does not mean stopping or giving up! It means that you accept that your practice is different each day and you continue on. You keep practicing. You accept that you have some limitations, but you do not let them stop you.

While this acceptance starts on your yoga mat, it will enter other areas of your life. There is freedom in discerning what you can change, what you can't, and moving forward with that knowledge.

Breath

Breath is the primary support for everything we do. The use of slow and conscious breathing balances the nervous system, initiates the relaxation response, and grounds us. The nervous system is further balanced as we use our breath in coordination with the yoga postures and movements.

Slow, steady, and even, with your mouth closed, is the way to breathe in your movement practice.

Calm and Supported Spine

Structurally, our spine contains and protects our central nervous system. With the practice of the *calm and supported spine* we facilitate healthy movement that doesn't disrupt the flow of the central nervous system or the health of the spine.

Imagine that you have a golden thread that runs right through the center of your body, from your pelvic floor to the crown of your head. Imagine that this thread is kept long and unbroken. You can bend forward and you can bend backward, but without loosening or breaking the thread. It stays long and strong. You can even spiral around it, but still it is unbroken.

Full Body Postures

You will explore the concept of *full body postures* in your asana practice. A full body posture means that you form a connection from your *feet to your head* and from your *hands to your tail*. From this connection of your feet fully on the earth, you follow the sensation of pressing your feet firmly into the earth and drawing your awareness upward, all the way through your body to the crown of your head. As you reach your arms upward, you follow the sensation from your hands all the way through you to your tail. Being mindful that the postures are full body postures and you are not just swinging your legs or arms around, you naturally begin to feel more connected to yourself and to your environment.

Each day that you step back onto your mat you find a little more of this support and integration and less fragmentation. This feeling of integration will bring you back to your mat day after day.

Navel Support

Imagine for just one moment that you or someone else has a supportive hand on your belly or right on your navel. Can you also imagine that this hand is very softly pressing inward to create support? Allow yourself to explore the sensation of how this would feel.

We will call this *navel support* and will ask that you try to maintain it throughout your practice. Navel support is very important because it maintains the integrity of your spine by keeping it long and ensuring that your lower back does not collapse. This support also teaches you to pay attention and helps to keep you in the present moment.

Yield—An Active Relationship with Earth

Yielding into the earth or *grounding* is one of the very first supports we explore. Like everything in life, it's important to know that you have the support you need before you move forward. We have provided specific postures and techniques to help you find a connection to earth with your feet, and even with your hands when they are on the earth. This grounding connection to earth lets us know that we have the support we need to move forward safely and with stability. This earthy, grounded feeling, or yielding into the earth, provides steadiness accompanied by a calm presence and sense of ease. With continued practice, you may find a new sensation of having support under you in many different areas of your body. You may even begin to spontaneously initiate movement from these supports. When you know where your support is coming from, you find comfort.

Finding this connection, or relationship with earth, may help you begin to find a renewed relationship with yourself. Finding and nurturing this relationship with yourself and feeling fully supported by the earth under you will also allow you to begin to explore your relationship with others. Yoga offers us choice in our actions. Each of us takes our own time in coming into a different relationship with self, earth, and others. There is no timetable except for your own comfort. You are the boss in this.

Yoga Props

The use of props can be a very helpful way to enhance your yoga practice. In this practice guide we give you the option of using them.

Yoga Mat — Your mat is probably the most important of all props because it keeps you from slipping and sliding. Mats come in many sizes, colors, and textures. It all boils down to personal preference. You will be placing your feet, your hands, and sometimes your face on your mat, so it would be better to buy your own mat instead of using the community mats in the yoga centers.

Yoga Blocks — Your block can be used in many different ways. Support for your hands in standing postures, forward bends, and twists are a few examples. You may also sit on your block and use it for some inversion postures.

Yoga Strap — Your yoga strap can be used to help you reach your feet in postures when you are unable to. It can also help to maintain the integrity of a posture.

Blankets—Blankets can be used as support in many ways depending on the way that they are folded or rolled.

Cushions—Cushions are used to find comfort in a seated posture while practicing meditation or breathing practices. Some cushions are filled with cotton and some filled with buckwheat hulls.

A daily asana or mindful movement practice is recommended, but a few times a week could be a very good way to begin.

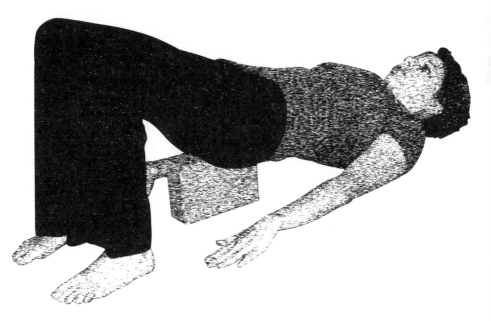

Mindful Movement or Asana Practice

Breathing

Constructive Rest

Begin by lying down on the floor in **Constructive Rest**. (Lie on your back with your knees bent and your feet on the floor hips distance apart. Allow your knees to rest together.)

Continue here with one of the breathing practices (**Cellular Breath** or **Three-part Breath**). Spend about 5 to 15 minutes here. This is a good time to pay attention to being present and to notice that the breath is the tool to help you with that.

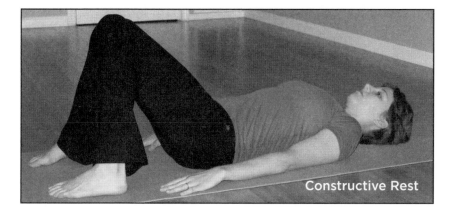

Constructive Rest

Moving Warm-up

Begin to use your **Victorious Breath** (Ujjayi Breath) (see page 18).

Start your movement by bringing your knees hips width apart as you prepare for **Bridge.** Just notice your feet on the earth. Place your hands, palms down, on the earth by your sides. Press into the earth with your feet and hands. These connections help to ground you. As you press your feet and hands into the earth, with an inhale lift your hips off the floor and come to the tops of your shoulders. Then with your exhale slowly lower down—one vertebra at a time—beginning with your upper back, through the mid-back, and finally

Bridge

your lower back and hips. *Repeat Bridge 3 times,* inhaling each time you press down to lift up, and exhaling each time you slowly roll back down.

On an exhale, bring your **Knees to Chest** and give them a little squeeze. If it is comfortable for you, you may also roll your knees from side to side as you continue to inhale and exhale.

Knees to Chest

When you are ready, roll over to your side and come to your **Hands and Knees**. Place your hands slightly forward of your shoulders, and your knees directly under your hips. Bring your attention to your hands. Allow the hands to yield into the earth and let this keep you grounded and present. Softly bend your elbows and press the entire surface of each of your hands into the earth. As you press into your hands and connect with earth, see if you can feel the rebound of that connection all the way up through your body and to your tailbone.

Next, imagine that you have your hand on your navel. Imagine that this hand supports you from the underside of your body. This is called *navel support*. Navel support allows the spine to be long

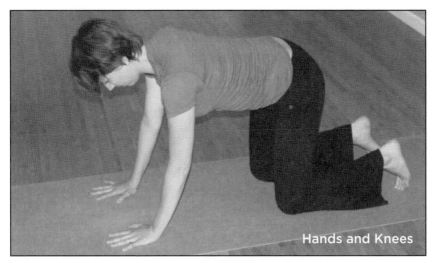

Hands and Knees

and supported, protecting and strengthening the lower back. We encourage you to maintain this support throughout your practice.

With an inhale, maintaining this navel support, raise your right arm and left leg into **Hands and Knees Balance**. Reach them in opposite directions. Your hand will be reaching forward and your leg reaching behind you. Remember this is just an exploration. This is not about doing something right or wrong. Continue to explore your supports.

Hands and Knees Balance

The grounding of the opposite hand and leg that are pressing into the earth and the navel support should keep you steady and even. Remain here for 5 breaths and then exhale as you draw them back down and place them on the earth. *Repeat other side.*

Press your hands into the earth as you exhale and press back into **Wisdom Pose**. See if you can notice the even connection from the press of the hands all the way through to your tailbone. *Take 3 breaths here.*

Wisdom Pose

Keeping your lower legs on the earth, inhale and draw your body toward your hands, staying low. Push with your hands as you draw yourself forward and upward into **Cobra**, while widening your collarbones and keeping your elbows tucked right beside your body.

Cobra

Repeat Wisdom Pose and Cobra a few times.

Keeping your hands directly under your shoulders, yielding into the earth and pressing your hands fully into the earth, roll your toes under, bend your knees, and push back into **Downward Facing Dog**. From this firm press of your hands see if you can draw your awareness all the way through to your sitting bones and tail-bone. Maintain your navel support and a soft bend in your knees. Lengthen both sides of your waist. If you have tight hamstrings, feel free to bend your knees even more.

Downward Facing Dog

From here, walk your hands to your feet or your feet to your hands.

Standing Forward Bend

When you have arrived, exhale all the way over into a **Standing Forward Bend** with your knees bent or soft (not locked).

Inhale and come up to standing, reaching your arms toward the sky, and then exhale your arms down by your sides to **Mountain**. This is a very good place to explore the subtle connections throughout your body.

Spend a couple of minutes here in **Mountain**. Start with your feet hips distance apart. Softening your knees, let the whole bottom of each foot hug the earth. While pressing your feet into the earth, draw your awareness all the way upward through you until you reach the top of your head. Your ankles, hips, and shoulders should arranged one over the other. Bring back the imaginary hand on

Mountain

Reach Up

your navel and look for support in that area. Another reminder: try to maintain these supports all the way through the practice. If you forget, it's OK. Practice acceptance and find the supports again.

Take a few additional breaths. Explore yielding and the connection you have with the ground as you press your feet into the earth.

Let's continue to connect movement with breath.

With an inhale, reach through your arms as they rise upward. Exhale and pull them back down by your sides. Fill your body with breath with each inhale. Remember to keep your mouth closed and breathe through your nose as much as possible. *Repeat 3 times.*

Sun Salutation

Begin in **Mountain**.

Press your feet into the earth, inhale and **Reach Up**.

Exhale into **Standing Forward Bend**, bending your knees so that you can place your hands on the floor.

On an inhale, maintain navel support as you lengthen out halfway, coming into **Half Standing Forward Bend**.

Standing Forward Bend | Half Standing Forward Bend

Bring your hands to the floor, exhale and step back into **Plank.** Your hands should be directly under your shoulders and your body in one long, even line. Feel the press of your hands all the way through to your tailbone and the connection from your feet all the way through to your head. The support in this posture comes from the underside of the body—your navel support. Keep your chest and collarbones wide. Be careful not to let your hips hang.

Inhale in **Plank**.

Plank

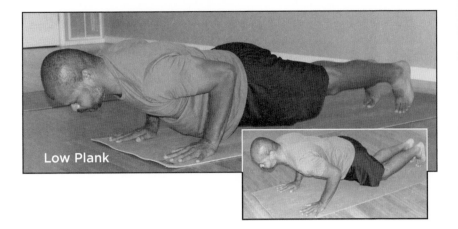

Low Plank

Exhale and lower down halfway to **Low Plank**. Or, you may use the modified version by putting your knees down and lowering your upper body half way down. Be sure to keep your elbows very close to your body and do not let your chest drop lower than your buttocks. This posture can be very challenging.

Inhale your way into **Upward Facing Dog**. The tops of the feet and the hands yield firmly into the earth as you draw yourself forward and upward. This posture is very similar to Cobra except that in Upward Facing Dog the tops of your feet are pressing into the earth and your legs and hips are off the floor. As in Cobra, chest and collarbones remain wide and the support comes from the underside of the body.

Upward Facing Dog

Downward Facing Dog

Exhale to **Downward Facing Dog**. *Take 3–5 breaths here.*

Exhale fully and step your feet forward to your hands. Inhale as you arrive in **Half Standing Forward Bend**. As you reach the crown of your head away, your spine lengthens out into its own neutral curves. Maintaining your navel support will help that. You have the option of keeping your knees soft or even bending them if you feel a tugging on your hamstrings.

Exhale and fold into a **Standing Forward Bend**.

Half Standing Forward Bend

Standing Forward Bend

Inhale and come up **Reaching Up**.

Exhale to **Mountain**.

Reach Up

Mountain

Repeat this Sun Salutation 3 times.

Standing Postures

Step out sideways on your mat with your legs wider than hips distance. Establish all the same supports that you have used previously to keep you feeling grounded—the press of the feet into the earth and maintaining your navel support.

Warrior

Warrior—Begin by spinning your right leg and foot out to the right. Turn your back leg and foot in a little bit. Line up your right heel with the arch of your left foot. Become really planted on the earth through your legs and feet! Inhale and reach your arms over your head. On an exhale, bend your right knee and slide your right sitting bone toward your right foot. Be careful not to let your knee go further forward than your ankle. Stay really stable through your back leg. Remember, this is a very strong and focused posture.

Take 3-5 breaths here. Maintain the supports that keep you grounded. Inhale and push into the earth to straighten your right leg and come out of the posture. Exhale your way back to center. *Repeat this on your left side.*

Triangle—Spin the right leg and foot out again, and be sure to line your feet up in the same way you did in the warrior posture. Inhale and reach your arms out to the sides, and as you exhale lightly bend the right knee. On your next inhale, begin to reach out over your right leg through your right arm—drawing your fingers and hands out and away. As you press your feet into the earth, draw

Triangle with Block

Triangle

your awareness all the way through to the top of your head. As you exhale, lengthen your right side body out over your right leg. Extend your right hand down toward your block or your shin. Let your left arm reach straight up toward the sky, with your left thumb directly over your mouth. *Take 3–5 breaths here.* Then, as you inhale, push into the earth and reach through your arms to come up. Your exhale will bring you back to center. ***Repeat on your left side.***

Come back to standing wide-legged on your mat with your feet parallel to the short edge of your mat and wider than your shoulders.

Standing Wide Leg Forward Bend—Place your hands on your hips and take an inhale. Exhale to lengthen your way forward and place your hands on the floor, right between your feet. Inhale and lengthen out half way, and then exhale and fold over. Your hands remain shoulder distance apart. Keep your elbows the same width as your hands. *Take 3–5 breaths here.* Then inhale and lengthen out half way to neutral curves of the spine. Exhale and place your hands on your hips, pressing your feet into the earth and using navel support. Inhale as you come all the way back up.

Wide-Legged Standing

Standing Wide Leg Forward Bend

Side Angle

Side Angle and Revolved Side Angle—Repeat the same alignment of your feet as in Warrior and Triangle, beginning on the right side. Inhale and reach your arms out to the sides. As you exhale, bend your right knee. Inhale again. As you exhale, bring your right forearm to your right thigh and reach your left arm all the way over your head for **Side Angle**. Be mindful not to collapse onto your right leg. Maintain the reach of your left arm and the support of the underside of your body. Keep your collarbones wide, so as not to collapse in your chest. *Take 3–5 breaths.* Inhale and come back up to center, going right to the next posture on this side.

Revolved Side Angle Variations

Exhale, spin your right foot forward, and take your left knee to the earth. As you inhale again, reach your left arm straight up in the air, lengthening the whole left side of your body. Exhale and hook your left elbow around your right knee. Press your palms firmly together and spiral toward the right. You can stay here in a **Revolved Side Angle** with your knee down. Or you can turn the toes of your left foot under, and bring your left knee up into a **Revolved Side Angle**. *Take 3–5 full breaths here.* Inhale and exhale as you release this posture. Inhale again and come up through center.

Repeat Side Angle and Revolved Side Angle on the other side.

Balancing

Tree—To balance in a posture it is helpful to be calm, steady, and focused. Remember that your even and steady breath is one of the tools that helps you stay calm and in the present moment.

Keep your gaze fixed on one point to help you be steady and calm. Press both feet firmly into the earth while drawing your awareness up to the crown of your head. Notice whether you still have navel support. Bring your right foot up and press it against your left leg. You can bring your foot above your knee or below your knee. You can even keep your toes on the floor if needed. Be mindful not to press your foot against your knee. Press your foot into your leg and press your leg into your foot, yielding into the earth again. Press your palms together in front of your heart. You can stay here, or you can reach your arms up as if they were limbs on a tree growing toward the sun. Try to stay calm and steady by focusing on your gazing point and your breath, even if your tree sways a little. *Take 5–10 breaths.*

Your exhale brings you back to **Mountain**. *Repeat on the left side.*

Tree   Tree   Mountain

Seated and Reclined Postures

From **Mountain**, with your feet pressing into the earth, inhale and reach up. Exhale and fold forward, placing your hands on the floor,

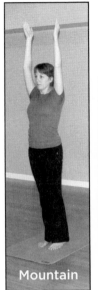

and step back into **Plank**. Inhale, and as you exhale this time lower yourself all the way to the floor (belly down).

Mountain

Plank

Locust—Extend your arms alongside your body and press the backs of your hands into the earth. Remember to maintain your navel support. This is very important here because it supports the spine from the underside. It should feel as if someone has their hand on your belly and is lightly pressing inward. On the next inhale, lift and extend your feet and upper body at the same time. You are not just lifting your feet and body up—you are extending them in opposite directions. This creates space in the spine. You

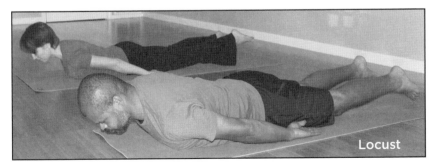

Locust

don't have to lift very high but you should try to reach your head and shoulders in one direction and your feet in the other. Remember to keep your inhale and exhale even. *Take 5 breaths here, then lower down on an exhale. Repeat this 3 times.*

Downward Facing Dog

Press the palms of your hands on the earth under your shoulders, and come to hands and knees. Exhale as you press back into **Downward Facing Dog**. *Take 3–5 breaths.* Inhale and come back to hands and knees, and then come to sitting on your mat.

Boat—In a seated position, place both of your feet on the floor. Place your hands behind your knees and lengthen your spine by drawing your awareness up toward the top of your head. Next reach your arms forward, and scoop your belly inward. Lift your feet off the floor and reach them away from you. Do not let your lower back collapse. Keep the crown of your head reaching upward. You may keep your knees bent or extend your legs until your toes are at eye level. If your lower back continues to collapse, just lift one leg. *Take 3–5 breaths.* On an exhale, bring your feet back to the floor. *Repeat. If you are lifting one leg, be sure to lift the other leg the second time.*

Boat

Boat

Boat

Seated Half Forward Bend—If you have tight hamstrings you may use a strap in this posture and you may even place a support (such as a blanket) under your sitting bones to lift you slightly. Optimally, you want to be seated right on the center of your sitting bones. Extend your left leg and place your right foot against your left thigh. Press your foot firmly into your thigh and let your thigh press back the same way you did in Tree. Inhale and reach for your left foot or your shin. You can even place a strap around your foot and reach for the strap. This is a really nice variation for tight hamstrings. Maintain the integrity of your spine by reaching through the crown of your head. Try to keep as much length in your spine as possible; it can be really easy to collapse here. Then, as you exhale, fold toward your left leg. *Take 5 breaths here.* Inhale and come back to center and exhale to release. *Repeat on the other side.*

Seated Half Forward Bend Variations

Supported Bridge—Lie down on your back with your feet on the earth and your feet and knees hips distance apart. Draw your heels back toward your sitting bones. Inhale and press your feet into the earth as you press your hips upward. As you bring your hips up and roll onto the tops of your shoulders, place your block under your sacrum. *The sacrum is the solid bone at the base of the spine, below the lumbar curve and between the sacroiliac joints. The block should feel comfortable here.*

Supported Bridge

The block can be used at three different heights. Flat on its wide side is the lowest height. The skinny long side is the next step up. The skinny short side is the highest.

Once you have the block under your sacrum, place your hands back on the floor alongside your body and press them firmly into the earth. Draw your chin toward your chest and do not turn your head from side to side. Inhale, and as you exhale draw your right knee in toward your chest. On your next inhale extend your right leg straight up in the air. *Take 3-5 breaths here.*

Inhale again, and as you exhale this time draw your right knee back in toward your chest. Your next inhale will bring your right foot back to the earth. Inhale again, and as you exhale draw your left in toward your chest. Inhale and extend your left leg upward. *Take 3-5 breaths here.* Inhale and exhale, drawing your left knee in toward your chest. Leave your left knee here and draw your right knee in as well. Both feet will be off the floor so be sure that you are supporting yourself with your hands as well as the block.

Supported Bridge

The next time you inhale, extend both legs upward. *Take at least 5 breaths here.* After taking the last breath, inhale, then exhale as you draw your knees in toward your chest. Inhale and place both feet back on the floor. Press both feet into the earth and come up just a little higher, then remove the block from under your sacrum. Inhale, reach your arms over your head, and as you exhale lower your back to the floor—one vertebra at a time, starting at the shoulders, and then the mid-back, and finally the lower back.

Take a moment here to let your spine settle.

Rest

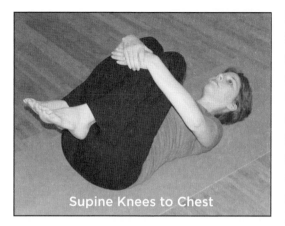

Supine Knees to Chest

Draw your knees in toward your chest again, and wrap your arms around them. With your knees still close to your chest, place your right hand on your left knee and extend your left arm straight out to the left. Inhale, and as you exhale roll your knees to the right. Take several breaths here. Inhale and draw your knees back to center, and exhale as you squeeze them back in toward your chest. Inhale and reach for your right knee with your left hand. Extend your right arm out to the right and exhale your knees all the way over to the left. Take several breaths here. Inhale and bring your knees back to center and squeeze in one more time. Exhale and release your feet to the earth.

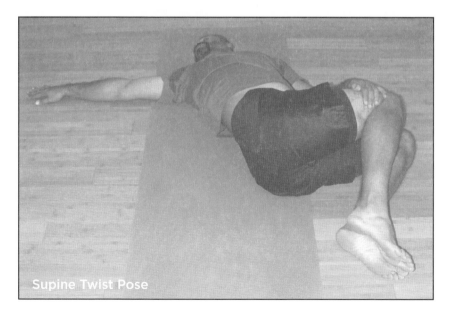

Supine Twist Pose

Rest

For rest you may lie on your back with your legs and arms extended, or you may find the posture that is most comfortable for you. If you would like to close your eyes, you may do so now, or just soften and rest your eyes.

Rest

Spend 5 to 10 minutes resting and absorbing the work you have done.

This practice is presented in pictures only at the end of the manual.

Yoga Nidra

Yoga Nidra is a practice that leads us into the deepest levels of relaxation in body and mind. The restfulness achieved in Yoga Nidra can be far more effective than the rest achieved in our conventional sleep. The total relaxation achieved in a yoga nidra session can be equivalent to hours of ordinary sleep and is profoundly rejuvenating for the body and nervous system. This technique is the jewel of yoga practice and anyone can do it.

The practice is found in the transitional space between sleep and waking. This is the place of clarity where wisdom is discovered. It's a place, we can learn to be present. Fear arises when we live in the future. The future is only a figment of our imagination. We really don't know what will happen next. Regret and reactiveness arrived from living in the past. The past is now a memory. We can't go back. We can only live in the present. Many of us are stuck in the past or constantly worried about the future. Yoga nidra helps us access the clarity and wisdom that can help us to stay in the present.

It is common to notice physical shifts or jumps in the body during the practice. This means negative patterns are being released as we tap into our natural, restful wisdom.

Systematic practice of yoga nidra may improve the health of the nervous system. The more frequently you use this practice, the more quickly you will notice its effects. A daily practice is highly recommended.

Yoga nidra has been used for a multitude of imbalances, ranging from simple relaxation, to insomnia, trauma, anxiety, fear, and depression. In order to harmonize our own body and mind, we need to find peace from within. Yoga nidra is a major key to finding this peace. The modern world is full of overstimulation and we are rewarded for multi-tasking. This ancient practice can be of huge benefit in a modern world.

Please use the information on the inside of the back cover to download this practice or stream from our website the yoga nidra practice by Patty Townsend. This practice is from her CD, "**Yoga Nidra with Patty Townsend**."

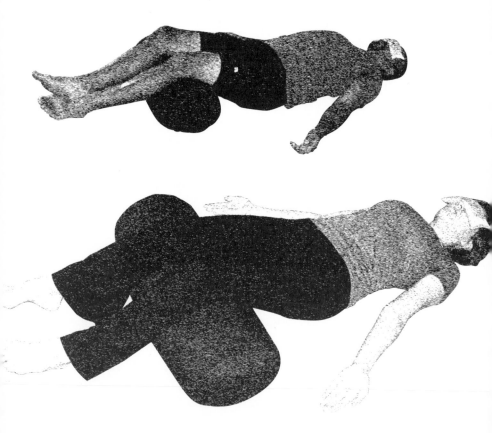

Meditation

Meditation is a practice through which we can become better acquainted with our own mental processes and therefore with our self. The mind can be a great source of distress when it is out of our control. When we cannot slow it down, or direct it, the mind becomes a source of anguish and frustration. The practice of meditation allows us to gain control of this so that we can use it to our benefit instead of allowing it to cause us distress. The practice of meditation allows us to find clarity, peace, and ultimate freedom.

Sample Meditation Practice

Find a comfortable seated position. You can sit on a cushion on the floor or on a chair. If you sit in a chair, you are encouraged to make sure that your feet are flat on the floor and connecting you to earth. Sit forward on the chair, so that you are not leaning back onto the chair, collapsing your spine, or rounding your low back or shoulders. If you are sitting on the floor, you can sit on a cushion with your legs crossed in front of you, and you can even sit with your back against the wall. What is most important is to find a position, which will allow you to feel comfortable with your spine supported and alert.

Rest your hands wherever it feels best. Options include in your lap, or one hand on each leg. If you can comfortably close your eyes, please do so. If not, please soften your gaze.

Then, when you are comfortable and ready, bring your complete attention to the sensation of your breath. Feel the breath inside your nostrils. Notice the pure sensations of each inhale and each exhale. You may notice the breath feels cool on the way in and warm on the way out. You may notice it feels soft and fuzzy like cotton or even has a velvety quality. You may also notice that it swirls on the way in. Just allow this breath and sensation without changing or judging it. Simply observe and accept this experience, as it feels right now, in this moment.

At some point it is likely that you will find that your mind has wandered away from the breath. This is to be expected. It is the nature of the mind to wander and its job to think. But we can become aware that the mind has wandered, maybe even note where it went, and then gently, without judgment, bring our attention back to the inhale and exhale, and the pure sensation of the breath. Instead of judging yourself or your thoughts when you find that the mind has wandered, each time just simply allow your attention to return back to the breath in this moment.

When you begin this practice, you may start by sitting for 10–15 minutes. Eventually you may want to grow into a 30-minute practice.

The sample mediation is on the **"Breathe In, Breathe Out"** CD. You can find instructions on the back inside cover on how to download this practice or stream it from the website.

The Practice of Gratitude

This very simple practice starts with just being grateful for what we have in our lives. Try taking a moment each day to acknowledge one thing that you are grateful for. As you practice, your focus will shift. Maybe the glass will be half full instead of half empty. It may get difficult when life presents its challenges, but this practice can change your outlook and the way that you move through life.

Start by pressing the palms of your hands together in front of your heart. Drop your gaze or take a slight bow with your head. See if this helps you arrive at a place that feels like gratitude. As you arrive there, think of one thing in your life today that you are truly grateful for and acknowledge it silently.

Try to carry this feeling with you throughout your day.

A Final Word

This guide is designed to help you discover the practices of yoga. It's normal to feel skeptical about starting yoga. After all, it's new and unfamiliar. Talking with other veterans who practice yoga, asking questions, and reading or researching online may help you gain a better understanding. You may locate a yoga class for veterans at a local VA, Veterans Center our your local yoga center. We encourage you to try several different yoga classes in your community. There are many different styles of yoga. While one may not resonate with you, another will. Don't be turned off by the ones that don't; keep trying classes and teachers until you find the place that feels correct for you. Once you start a practice, it's important to give it some time; results are not immediate. That's why it's called a practice. The positive results may surprise you and may be well worth the effort.

Glossary

Many yoga teachers teach using the language of Sanskrit. We thought it would be helpful to include some of the commonly used words so that if you ever decide to go to a yoga class in your community, you would not feel lost or uncomfortable. Sanskrit is just another language, nothing creepy.

Yoga is not a religion. However, it does seem to help us find a connection with body, mind, and spirit.

Asana
Asana is the name of the practice of the postures, or the postures connected to breath with movement in a steady and comfortable way.

Namaste
Pronounced na-ma-stay. *Namaste* is usually used as a greeting or when someone is leaving. It means, "The light in me honors the light in you."

Om
Om is said to be the sound of the vibration of the universe. Some yoga classes will chant the word Om before or after a class. They are acknowledging the sound of the universe.

Pranayama
The Sanskrit name for the breathing practices. *Prana* means life-force or breath-of-life and *ayama* means to stretch or extend. *Pranayama* is the practice of moving our breath through our body. There are many ways to practice pranayama and in fact Tactical Breathing may be one you are already acquainted with. Some practices are very strong and build heat, and others are softer and calming. The practices in this guide and on your "**Breathe In, Breathe Out**" CD are the pranayama practices we recommend for veterans recovering from PTS.

Ujjayi

Ujjayi means "victorious" breath but is sometimes is called "ocean breath" because it sounds like the ocean. Creating a slight constriction at the back of the throat while the mouth is closed makes this sound. By doing this we are able to sip the breath in slowly and create better absorption and balance in the nervous system. You are encouraged to create an even length for the inhale and the exhale. You want to breathe in as much breath as you breathe out

Yoga

The word *yoga* means "union." It's an ancient discipline that consists of many practices including breathing practices, movement and postures, yoga nidra, meditation and mindfulness. It is not a religion or an exercise program. As we learn to direct the breath, we begin to unite body and mind, and we become whole, and find peace.

Mindful Movement Asana Practice (Pictures Only)

Below is the mindful movement asana practice presented in pictures only. As you become familiar with the practice, you may want to use just these pictures to guide you.

Moving Warm-Up

Sun Salutation

Practice the rows of postures from left to right.

Standing Postures

Balance

Seated and Reclined Postures

Rest

Practice the rows of postures from left to right.

63

About the Authors

Suzanne Manafort, ERYT 500, is the Director of Newington Yoga Center in Newington, CT and Founder of Mindful Yoga Therapy.

 She has studied extensively with Beryl Bender Birch in the Hard and Soft Yoga Institute and also with Patty Townsend in the Embodyoga® Teacher Training programs. She is now on faculty in both schools and teaches in both teacher training programs. At the Himalayan Institute, Suzanne completed the yearlong Living Tantra Program and the Sage Program taught by Pandit Rajmani Tigunait.

She has worked with veterans who suffer with PTS for many years. This work led her to study and learn the practical supports and benefits that veteran's receive in a yoga program. Her experiences along the way have taught her that teachers require additional training tailored to the specific needs of veterans.

Suzanne co-authored *Mindful Yoga Therapy* Practice Guide. She also produced three CDs—*Yoga Nidra by Suzanne Manafort*, *"Breathe, In Breathe Out"* and *Resilience*.

Suzanne is on the Board of Directors of the Give Back Yoga Foundation. In 2009, she was designated a Wells Fargo Second Half Champion for her work with veterans.

Robin Gilmartin is a licensed clinical social worker specializing in treatment of anxiety disorders and PTSD. She has worked with veterans at the Newington, Connecticut and West Haven, Connecticut VA hospitals for 18 years. Robin was Director of the PTSD Residential Treatment Program for 9 years, a program of national prominence that serves men and women returning from Iraq and Afghanistan.

In early 2013, she opened a general psychotherapy practice in West Hartford, CT while also continuing to work with veterans and their families through Connecticut's Military Support Program.

Robin is a graduate of Smith College School for Social Work and has published and presented on topics ranging from personal narratives of the mentally ill, meaning-focused treatment for PTSD, and use of complementary therapies such as yoga and volunteer work in treating veterans with PTSD. She has been adjunct faculty at Smith College School for Social Work, University of Connecticut and Springfield College and enjoys training clinicians.

TESTIMONIALS

I recently had the opportunity to attend a series of classes at my local VA Hospital titled Mindful Yoga Therapy that was presented by Suzanne Manafort. I'd like to a minute to describe my experience.

The class met twice a week for twelve weeks and was attend by both men and women of various ages with military service dating from Viet Nam to present day conflicts. One thing we all had in common is that we are all under treatment for, and suffering from, Post Traumatic Stress Disorder and needed a doctor's referral to attend.

The vast majority of people who were in the class I attend had zero experience with both yoga and meditation, but all were willing to try something new to relieve some of the symptoms they were suffering from which the drugs/therapy currently available don't help with. While I describe my own experience in a minute, I just wanted to mention what I observed and heard from the others in the class.

One big thing that I noticed from the first class to the last was how much more flexible everyone was during the last class compared to the first. In general they were probably not as physically fit as they could have been at the start but there was a definite improvement by the end of the twelve weeks. The other thing, probably far more important to them getting into shape, was there mental state from beginning to end. I don't know how many times I heard someone mention in class that they were sleeping much better (a serious problem with PTSD) and one or more of their other symptoms were far less troubling. That to me was the whole reason behind the class, to show people there is a drug-free way to make them feel better, something they could do in the comfort of their own home and with a regular class for guidance and motivation. So to me, from what I saw and heard, the class was a great success.

As for myself, I spend a couple of years in Viet Nam and got out with a case of PTSD, but didn't realize it until years later. I had serious alcohol and drug problems, went from one relationship and job to another, barely got by financially, and watched helplessly as my life rapidly spiraled downward. Then one day at yet another job, in another town and in a rare lucid state, I ran across a paperback book, bought it, and my life changed forever. The book was a twenty-eight-day progressive yoga/meditation routine (similar to Mindful Yoga Therapy). By the time I was through with the book meditation had become a daily habit for me, one that has lasted for close to forty years. The drug and alcohol use had completely stopped, I became what people used to describe as a "health nut", gulping down vitamins, eating health food, becoming a vegetarian, and exercising daily. My entire life changed for the better with that book and continues to to this day. I went from someone who was a drug abusing, broke, depressed, and often homeless person to someone who has had many amazing adventures and a very interesting and productive life. I retired in my fifties, am financially secure, and continue to improve myself and try to help others in the process, recently becoming an EMT and soon attending advanced Paramedic training. I can't honestly say the yoga and meditation cured me of PTSD completely, I still see a therapist and I've hit a few rough spots along the way, but I CAN say without a doubt that if I hadn't started meditating years ago I could pretty much guarantee you that I'd be dead or in prison by now. And I did it all without a single prescribed medication, solely with yoga and meditation. Lastly, I wanted to mention that even with all the previous experience I had with meditation even I noticed a definite improvement in my mental state while and after taking this class.

Mindful Meditation (and similar practices) are a great way to treat the symptoms of PTSD. I know it works, I'm living proof of that and I'm certain there are other stories such as mine out there. I urge you to not only continue this program, but to expand it throughout the VA system. Military personnel are putting their lives on the line every day for this country and I think the least the government can do in return is to do everything possible to heal us once we come home. This program is a cheap, side-effect free, safe, and effective way to do just that.

—Joseph

I am a Iraq war Veteran who works as a Peer Support Specialist. Also, I suffer from PTSD, anxiety, panic attacks and I have a mild TBI. Before working here in December 2012, I found your website and received the Mindful Yoga Therapy for Veterans Recovering from Trauma book w/cds. That book helped me deal with my symptoms and I found out that I like to do yoga and meditation, two things I never thought I would do.

Now that I work here at the VA, I'm trying to help my fellow Veterans gain the same relief and peace that I felt from this program. I am able to run groups here and one of them is a stress/anxiety management group. Is there a way that I can get the book in bulk for the program? I think it would be a great tool for the Veterans to have to take home with them.

Thank you for this program, it helped give me life again.

—Melanie, Peer Support Specialist, Iraq War Veteran

I always knew I wanted my yoga work to be something purposeful and authentic. In the process of being trained in Mindful Yoga Therapy for Veterans, I realized this program would have a profound impact on other populations that suffered with PTSD and trauma. Working with female Domestic Violence and Sexual Abuse survivors, applying the MYT protocol to create a safe space for women has been deeply satisfying.

I have been able to give my students a toolbox to cope with their domestic violence and sexual abuse trauma that has had profound and subtle effects. From the manner in which they interact with others, to the way they carry their physical bodies and make eye contact, the differences are discernable. The breathing practices have aided in reducing their anxiety and depression. Over time, using the MYT protocol, my students have begun to exhibit a sense of empowerment and a calm radiance that was not present before. The practices of mindfulness and gratitude have been powerful in diminishing and healing the shame, fear and guilt that many survivors of domestic violence and sexual abuse struggle with. The practice of acceptance and non-judgment has set the foundation for rebuilding self-esteem and self-worth. It is an honor to see how these women, knowing the challenges they have endured, have begun the process of healing and developing a deeper connection with themselves through their participation in Mindful Yoga Therapy.

—Heather, MYT Teacher